Pursued by a Bear
Productions

## Pursued by a Bear Productions

**in association with BT Studio, Oxford Playhouse
and supported by the Mercury Theatre, Colchester
present:**

# KALASHNIKOV

## In the Woods by the Lake
### A play in eight parts
### By Fraser Grace

First performance at the Burton Taylor Studio,
Oxford Playhouse on Thursday 6th October 2011.

# KALASHNIKOV

## In the Woods by the Lake

**A play in eight parts**

**By Fraser Grace**

*Cast in order of appearance*

**KALASHNIKOV** | **ANDREW NEIL**
**MAKKA** | **MAGGIE O'BRIEN**
**VOLKOV** | **OWEN OAKESHOTT**
**ELENA** | **ANASTASIA DREW**

**DIRECTOR** | **HELENA BELL**
**DESIGNER** | **CHRISTOPHER FAULDS**
**FILMMAKER/LIGHTING DESIGN** | **DAVID RAFIQUE**
**FILMMAKER/SOUND DESIGN** | **GRANT WATSON**
**COMPANY STAGE MANAGER** | **NICOLA MADDOX**
**ASSISTANT TO THE PRODUCTION TEAM** | **POPPY SAKULKU**

**ADMINISTRATOR** | **JO TURNER**
**PRESS REPRESENTATIVE** | **SHERIDAN HUMPHREYS**
**RUSSIAN CONSULTANT** | **DR SVETLANA RESTON**
**GRAPHIC DESIGNER** | **DEBRA HUTCHINGS**
**PRODUCTION PHOTOGRAPHY** | **JEROME HUNT**
**ACCOUNTANT** | **CHARLES BARKER-BENFIELD**

**FOR PURSUED BY A BEAR PRODUCTIONS**

**ARTISTIC DIRECTOR** | **HELENA BELL**
**ASSOCIATE DIRECTOR (FILM)** | **GRANT WATSON**
**ADMINISTRATOR** | **JO TURNER**
**CREATIVE PRODUCER (FILM)** | **JANE McGIBBON**
**ASSOCIATE PLAYWRIGHT** | **OLADIPO AGBOLUAJE**

## THE COMPANY

**Fraser Grace,** *Writer*

**Writing for Theatre** includes: *Perpetua* (Birmingham REP/
Soho Theatre, joint winner of the Verity Bargate Award); *Gifts
of War* and *Frobisher's Gold* (Menagerie Theatre Company,
touring); *Who Killed Mr Drum?* (with Sylvester Stein, Treatment
Theatre/Riverside Studios); *Breakfast with Mugabe* (Royal
Shakespeare Company, joint winner of the John Whiting Award
2006); *The Lifesavers* (Theatre503/Mercury Theatre Colchester,
shortlisted for TMA Best Play 2009); *King David: Man of Blood*
(Mercury Theatre, Colchester, 2010).

**Writing for Radio** includes: *Bubble* (with Andrea Porter, R4);
*Breakfast with Mugabe*, (Silver Sony Award, R3 and the World
Service); *Wrestling Angels - 3 stories for radio* (R4).

Fraser teaches playwriting at Anglia Ruskin University,
Cambridge, and is the newly appointed co-ordinator of
the MPhil Playwriting Studies course at the University of
Birmingham. He is currently writing an opera with the
composer Andrew Lovett. Called *Don't Breathe A Word*, it was
recently showcased at the Linbury Studio, Covent Garden, and
continues to be developed with the Royal Opera House. His
plays are published by Oberon books.

**Andrew Neil,** *Kalashnikov*

Andrew trained at RADA. Seasons at Glasgow Citizens, Leicester Phoenix, the Royal Court and in the West End before directing in various reps and substantially at RADA and LAMDA. Head of Acting at the Welsh College of Music & Drama 1985-1996. Since returning to acting he has worked in London, Edinburgh, Stoke and Budapest. Television includes *Doctors; The Bill; Casualty; Taggart; Hotel Babylon* and *Rebus*. Films include *The Debt Collector; Savage; Man Hunter - The Wolf* and *Crying with Laughter*. He also played Almighty God in Fraser Grace's *King David: Man of Blood* in Colchester in 2010.

**Maggie O'Brien,** *Makka*

Theatre credits include: *He's Much to Blame* (Theatre Royal, Bury St Edmunds); *Faith Healer* (Salisbury Playhouse); *The Flying Machine* (Unicorn Theatre); *Be My Baby, Cider With Rosie* (New Vic, Stoke); *Beauty Queen of Leenane* (Bolton Octagon, MEN nominated); *Frozen* (London Classic Theatre); *Trashed* (Theatre Centre); *Topless Mum in Dead Hero Shocker* (Tobacco Factory); *Ship of Fools* (Theatre503); *Precious Bane* (Pentabus); *The Winter's Tale, As You Like It* (Shakespeare by the Sea, Sydney); *Caucasian Chalk Circle* (Theatre de Complicite/Royal National Theatre); *Don Juan* (Commotion); *Smashed Eggs* (Theatre Royal Northampton); *A Busy Day* (Show of Strength/ The King's Head Theatre); *The Kitchen* (Royal Court) and *Dancing at Lughnasa* (Palace Theatre Westcliff).

**Owen Oakeshott,** *Volkov*

Theatre credits include: *Desire Under the Elms* (New Vic Theatre, Newcastle); *Antony & Cleopatra* [Antony] (Nuffield Theatre); *Slaves* (Theatre503); *Copenhagen* (Royal Lyceum, Edinburgh); *Roots* (Manchester Royal Exchange); *The Oxford Passion* (Creation Theatre Company); *Bites* (The Bush Theatre); *Way Upstream* (Derby Playhouse); *Destiny* (BAC); *An Inspector Calls* (West End); at the National Theatre *The Royal Hunt of the Sun* and *Market Boy* and seasons at the RSC (*Richard III; Henry VI, Pts I, II & III; Antony & Cleopatra; Timon of Athens* and *The General from America*).

Television includes: *Trial & Retribution; Spooks; Dream Team; She's Gone; Bad Girls; Armadillo; Family Affairs; The Bill; The Professionals* and *Birds of a Feather*.

**Anastasia Drew,** *Elena (on film)*

Anastasia studies music, dance and acting at the ARTS Education school, London and has also studied the Stanislavsky system at the Russian theatre school RITS. She made her West End debut in the pantomime *Snow White and the Seven Dwarfs*. Anastasia, whose mother is Russian, speaks fluent Russian and is delighted to be part of *Kalashnikov*.

### Helena Bell, *Director*

Helena is the Artistic Director of Pursued by a Bear for whom she has produced and directed *Footprints in the Sand* by Oladipo Agboluaje and Rukhsana Ahmad (Oval House & South East tour) and *Fresh Tracks* - a festival of short, new plays. Prior to PBAB Helena was awarded a year-long Arts Council Directors' Bursary during which time she specialised in new writing productions. Helena went on to freelance as a Director/Dramaturg for Soho Theatre; Kali Theatre; New Writing South; Brighton Theatre Events; Oxford Touring Theatre Company; Theatre Centre; Trinity Arts Centre and the Mercury Theatre, Colchester. For ten years she was Co-Artistic Director of Brighton's Alarmist Theatre for whom she directed many new touring productions including *Fossil Woman* - Time Out Critics' Choice and transfer to Lyric Hammersmith; *The School of Night* (Croydon Warehouse) and *The Bedbug* - British Council tour to Moscow.

### Christopher Faulds, *Designer*

Christopher graduated in 2006 with a degree in Fine Art, specialising in sculpture and installation. He then went on to complete a MA in Theatre Design (Bristol Old Vic Theatre School). In 2009, he won the Jocelyn Herbert Award for theatre design and was also a Linbury Prize finalist.

Since then he has designed for theatre, ballet and still & moving image, both in the UK and abroad. Selected design credits include: *The Three Musketeers* (Unicorn Theatre); *Minor Sonata* (Mikhailovsky Theatre, St Petersburg and London Coliseum); *Visits* by Jon Fosse (Theatre Delicatessen, London) and *Unspoken Voices* (Arnolfini, Bristol).

http://www.theatredesign.org.uk/designer-pages/christopherfaulds/

**David Rafique,** *Filmmaker/Lighting Design*

David trained as a filmmaker at St Martins School of Art and as an actor at The City Lit Institute. In a varied career David has dovetailed cinematography with theatre lighting design, acting, screenwriting and producing/directing films and videos. As a cinematographer he has worked on productions ranging from corporate videos to pop promos to feature films. His most recent theatre work was creating the lighting for *The Ditch Digger* at The Arcola.

**Grant Watson,** *Filmmaker/Sound Design*

Grant is the Associate Director (Film) for Pursued by a Bear Productions. He trained on the MA in Theatre Arts at Essex University. He is a filmmaker, writer and director. Theatre credits include *Food* (Lyric Theatre, Hammersmith); *The Nativity* (Chapter Arts Centre, Cardiff) and most recently *The Art of Hiding* (Farnham Maltings). Television includes *Holby City* (BBC1); *Doctors* (BBC2) and *Family Affairs* (Channel 5). Grant has made a number of short films including *The North* and *The Horse Killer* (both for Pursued by a Bear) as well as *B Boy* (Creative Communities/Arts Council) and *Arcadia* (HarperCollins). Grant is currently developing a feature length screenplay for Pursued by a Bear.

**Nicola Maddox,** *Company Stage Manager*

Nicola has been a freelance technician and Stage Manager since graduating from University College London where she was an active member of the University's Stage Crew society. She was Technical Manager of The UCLU Garage Theatre Workshop 2007 – 2009, technician at Arcola Theatre, and, most recently, Technical Manager at C Soco in Edinburgh.

Stage Management credits include: *Jekyll and Hyde: The Musical*, *Jesus Christ Superstar* and *West Side Story* (UCLU @ The UCL Bloomsbury); *Knives in Hens*, *Boy With A Suitcase*, *The Savage*, *Under The Pillow* and *Doorway* (Arcola Theatre); *Aladdin, Jack and the Beanstalk, Stardust, Enfield School's Dance Festival* (Millfield Arts Centre); *Clockwork Orange* (Fourth Monkey) and *As We Forgive Them* (Ensemble52).

**Poppy Sakulku,** *Assistant to the Production Team*

Poppy graduated with a degree in English and Media Studies from Brighton University in 2010. Since then she has worked for Farnham Maltings as an Assistant Events Organiser and as an ASM (Wardrobe & Hair) for their outdoor Heritage production of *The Art of Hiding*. Prior to this she worked on location as a runner for PBAB's short film *The Horse Killer* and as a researcher for ALTO films in Brighton. Poppy is currently writing her own screenplay and is delighted to be gaining further experience in theatre and filmmaking on this production.

**Jo Turner,** *Administrator*

Jo has worked in marketing for the voluntary sector for over 10 years, and enjoyed her first role with Pursued by a Bear in 2008 when she worked on *Footprints in the Sand*. She is delighted to be part of *Kalashnikov* as she read Russian at university.

Pursued by a Bear
Productions

**Pursued by a Bear Productions** was formed in 1998 by director Stuart Mullins and actor Joseph Millson to produce the work of writer Craig Baxter who wrote *The Animals* (Dublin Theatre Festival), *Monogamy* (Riverside studios) and *The Ministry of Pleasure* (Theatre503).

These productions were followed by:

**2003:** *You Don't Kiss* by Troy Andrew Fairclough (Oval House and Tour): winner of the Newnham New Writing Award for Best New Play.

**2004:** *All Fall Away* by Said Sayrafiezadeh (Theatre503). [PBAB moves to Farnham Maltings as a Resident Company.]

**2005:** *Pieces of Me* by Hong Khaou (co- produced with the Chinese and Vietnamese communities on the Ferrier Estate in Greenwich).

**2006:** Alex Clifton joins as new Artistic Director. His production of *Yorgin Oxo - The Man* by Thomas Crowe (Theatre503) awarded Time Out Critics' Choice.

**2007:** Helena Bell joins as new Artistic Director with Grant Watson as Associate Director for film. The company specialise in the commissioning of UK writers to produce new plays with global themes.

**2008:** *Footprints in the Sand:* a double bill by Oladipo Agboluaje (*For One Night Only*) and Rukhsana Ahmad (*Letting Go*) explores the dreams and aspirations of African refugees in Britain (Oval House & South East Tour).

**2009:** *Fresh Tracks:* a playwriting award for six promising young writers from the South East (Farnham Maltings).

**2010:** The commissioning and development of Fraser Grace's *Kalashnikov* and Satinder Chohan's *Kabaddi-Kabaddi-Kabaddi* – an Olympic-themed play set in India, 1936 and London, 2012.

**2011** Fraser Grace and Helena Bell awarded an Arts Council research & development grant to visit Moscow and Kalashnikov's hometown of Izhevsk (also home to the national Kalashnikov Museum).

## Pursued by a Bear Productions

Farnham Maltings, Bridge Square, Farnham, Surrey, GU9 7QR

Telephone: 01252 745 445

Email: pursuedbyabear@yahoo.co.uk

Website: www.pursuedbyabear.co.uk

Registered company: 3800928 / Registered charity: 1091842

*Pursued by a Bear Productions* would like to say thank you to: Jenny Roberts and Richard Kingdom at Arts Council South East; Isobel Hawson; British Council, Edinburgh Showcase 2011; Decibel Showcase 2011; Gavin Stride and Fiona Baxter at Farnham Maltings; Charlie Field and Robert Bristow at Burton Taylor Studio; Brian Kirk at Guildford's Yvonne Arnaud Theatre; Dee Evans, Adrian Grady and Tony Casement at the Mercury Theatre, Colchester; Jane Mackintosh at GLYPT; Captain Peter Laidler, The UK MOD (SASC – Small Arms Collection); New Writing South; Lyudmila Drew-Baranova; Jean Uren; Diane and Tony Watson; Uschi Gatward; Julian Freeman at Charterhouse; Jason Barningham at artsouk; SUPERHIGHCEILING for set construction; Dmitry at Peace Travel Services; Simon Hardwick at Chimaera Design Online; Joe Phillips at Curtis Brown and everyone at Oberon Books.

*Kalashnikov, In the Woods by the Lake, a play in eight parts,* was first developed and showcased at the Burton Taylor Studio, Oxford Playhouse in September 2010 with funding support by the National Lottery through Arts Council, England.

Pursued by a Bear
Productions

**LOTTERY FUNDED**

ARTS COUNCIL
ENGLAND

**BURTON TAYLOR
STUDIO**

mercurytheatre
COLCHESTER

farnham **maltings**

KALASHNIKOV: IN THE WOODS BY THE LAKE

Fraser Grace

# KALASHNIKOV: IN THE WOODS BY THE LAKE

a play in eight parts

OBERON BOOKS
LONDON

WWW.OBERONBOOKS.COM

First published in 2011 by Oberon Books Ltd
521 Caledonian Road, London N7 9RH
Tel: 020 7607 3637 / Fax: 020 7607 3629
e-mail: info@oberonbooks.com
www.oberonbooks.com

A catalogue record for this book is available from the British
Library.

ISBN: 978-1-84943-242-9

Cover design by Debra Hutchings

Printed and bound by CPI Group (UK) Ltd, Croydon, CR0 4YY.

in memory of Mervyn Uren

1922 – 2011

We are born in a clear field
and die in a dark forest.

Russian proverb

# Characters

KALASHNIKOV
an old man

MAKKA
his daughter, half his age

VOLKOV
no longer a young man

*ELENA
Kalashnikov's granddaughter


*the current script, specially commissioned by Pursued By A Bear Productions, assumes filmed sections in which ELENA appears.


*Author's Notes on Text.*

This is not a docudrama, more a creative investigation.

Mikhail Kalashnikov was born in 1919 and, when the play was written, was still alive and living in Izhevsk in the Russian Republic of Udmurtia. Any resemblance between Makka, Elena or Volkov and any real person, living or dead, is coincidental.

While both the history captured in the play, and the views expressed by the central character, are believed to be accurate, the events of the play are entirely fictitious.

Where words appear in brackets within a line, it indicates implicit meaning. Where it occurs after an ellipsis, it indicates where the line is headed. The actor concerned may use as much of this bracketed material as necessary – or possible, if cut off by the next line.

# Prologue

I

*Film: ELENA, a girl of about twelve years old, is glimpsed stealing through
thick forest. At length, having found a place to hide, she turns to us, puts
her finger to her lips, and signals we should not tell.*

II

*Stage: The garden of a dacha on a promising morning – the first time
in a long winter when spring seems a genuine possibility; snow on the
ground, the sky a bank of dull white cloud, just the hint of weak sunshine.
In the garden, a table, with bench seats. A line of washing.*

*Upstage, the dacha, and glimpsed beyond it, the lake, still frozen.*

*Offstage right, a path (leading to the gate, and to the lake road).*

*Stage left, a small wooden tool store, and beyond, offstage left, the forest.*

*KALASHNIKOV enters through the auditorium. We hear him before we
see him.*

KALASHNIKOV: ...nine hundred and ninety-seven, nine
      hundred and ninety-eight, nine hundred and ninety-
      nine...

    *Lights up on KALASHNIKOV, unshaven, wearing an old dressing
    gown, and medals.*

    ...a thousand.

*Beat. He calls into the forest.*

    ...Coming Elena, ready or not.

*He looks around at the audience, clearly making no move.*

    We should be clear:
    the world I loved

the club I was so eager to join
would have ditched me in a second
– god knows with what brutality! –
if it guessed the truth of my origins.
'Father' was a Kulak,
a small-time landowner.
In the view of the Soviet,
an insufficiently-impoverished peasant.

*He produces tobacco and papers, and begins to roll himself a cigarette.*

Imagine! Mother Russia's favourite soldier,
*Vrag naroda* – enemy of the people!
Forty years on that was still my secret.
How did you hide that one, Misha?

*Beat.*

The best way to hide anything in Russia
with medals,
and some modest achievements in the field of
engineering.

That world
my beloved Union of Soviet Socialist Republics
that's over now,
frittered away by the idiot Gorbachev.
This new world
this 'post-Soviet' Russia,
doesn't breed heroes,
has to keep rolling out the old ones.

Six times I was appointed to the Supreme Soviet! Six!
One thing you can say about Russia –
To be a representative of the people
is an undeniable honour.

*He refers to his medals.*

'Hero of Soviet Labour', that's me
twice-over. I was also named
Best Industrial Entrepreneur Number Two
by Gorbachev!
No prizes for guessing
Best Industrial Entrepreneur Number One.

*He mouths Gorbachev's name, then straightens himself up.*

I am General Mikhail Timofeyevich Kalashnikov –
Retired. Semi-retired, I live here by the lake.
Across the water,
the other side of that great mirror
within sight, within sound almost,
lies my darling – Izhmash:
the most beautiful Motor Factory in all the Russias.
You smile; good!
It's good to smile!
That factory, Izhmash – she is the nest,
the womb from which my baby
– my modest achievement in the field of engineering –
took off round the globe,
K for 'Kalashnikov'
stamped on every little arse.

India, Africa, the Central Asian Republics
places I'd never been,
never dreamed I'd be allowed to travel to.

Coca Cola, Nike, BMW…Kalashnikov;
Everywhere my name goes before me.
Without me, these days.

*He lights up.*

Motor Factory.
Another joke from the Soviet era.
We never built one tractor, one car

FRASER GRACE

in our part of the factory
not even one of your Toyotas!
Guns, since 1809 –
Since 1947, the Kalashnikov assault rifle
Avtomat Kalashnikova
AK-47 – d'you see?
Wait here.

*He goes into the dacha and returns briskly with an AK47. He is completely uninhibited in his handling of the gun, so that for a second, the man walking towards us loading his machine gun is threatening (sound might be amplified) – though in fact he is not loading but dismantling it as he goes.*

KALASHNIKOV: Child's play.
A child can dismantle and reassemble my gun
in under two minutes.
Unless the child's an idiot.

*He holds up each part of the gun in turn, and 'assigns' each to a member of the audience.*

Magazine: Here,
Keep an eye on this would you?

*He is dismantling the gun, placing the parts in a semi-circle downstage, and addressing members of the audience.*

*(To another.)* For you? Top Cover:
Watch it, please.
*(To another.)* Return spring and rod:
Yours. I'll leave it here.
*(To another.)* Breech Block Carrier:
Madam,
Keep an eye on this prize.
Your responsibility, alright?
*(To another.)* the Breech Block itself:
For you, comrade… Here.
*(To another.)* Gas compression chamber:

24

Yours.
Ha! Lucky you were never arrested, Misha;
Look!
A few seconds, and Kalashnikov's in pieces! Ha!
*(To another.)* Fore-rod:
For you. Watch it, please.
*(To another.)* And the last one is yours.
The stock.

*He surveys the half-ring of parts.*

Now, pay attention.
I'm showing you what, if I may say, is the genius of our
design. You see?
Just a handful of parts, but
even when assembled,
everything has its own space –
 room is given around the parts,
 'As if each component
was suspended in air'
Dirt has nowhere left to lodge –
dust, ice, not a hope –
'The gun that keeps on firing'.
Unlike if I may say the gun
designed by my rival and eventual friend
in America, Mr Eugene Stoner:
The United States Army's M-16.
A fine man, Stoner, a gentleman, and a
good designer, but the M-16 in my opinion…
Well, in our tank unit we had a saying:
If it can rain, it will. So please, for the love of Stalin,
give us a gun that'll work when it's pissing down.
Besides
no one's going to put a weapon as ugly as the M-16 on
a t-shirt
much less a flag.

Eugene Stoner. Gone now,
like all the rest.
They do the AK you know. Put it on flags,
T-shirts too.
Who'd have thought –
Little Misha Kalashnikov – enemy of the people,
doyen of the fashion industry.

*Having laid all the parts out in a semi-circle along the downstage edge of the playing area, he picks up one of the pieces, and examines it critically, but with satisfaction.*

Eight parts.
A kind of a miracle.
Despite not being a believer
miracles have played a great part in my life.
Mother, an illiterate peasant woman,
was labelled a kulak; inevitable, her husband
owning one too many cows,
her brother being a priest.
She was exiled, widowed, impoverished,
still she gave birth eighteen times – eighteen!
Ten of her babies went back to god,
as they said then, eight survived.
I was Mother's favourite, number eight of eighteen,
though if you'd asked my brother – number ten –
he would have said he was the favourite
so, who knows.

It's probable Mother, through suffering,
discovered the secret of true humanity: make a person
feel they and only they matter,
matter more than anything else in life.
There is a component I may be missing.

Kalashnikov, in eight parts, Part Number One
Slaughter of the beasts.

*The sound of beasts – pigs, sheep, cattle – in terrible distress.*

*MAKKA enters from the dacha, carrying a washing basket.*

MAKKA: He's here.

KALASHNIKOV: Makka, my daughter
    – my eyes, my ears too.

MAKKA: Papa!

KALASHNIKOV: All that test-firing – deaf as a post now.

MAKKA: PAPA, HE'S COMING.

KALASHNIKOV: Yes yes.

*The sound has gone.*

KALASHNIKOV: Not too much sugar this time.

*Beat.*

KALASHNIKOV: What.

MAKKA: Wear it while he's here. Please.

KALASHNIKOV: Again. And don't whisper.

MAKKA: FOR ME, PAPA.

*Beat. He gives way, taking out the hearing aid, and putting it on, fiddling with its fitting and adjustment through the next lines. MAKKA begins taking in the washing from the line.*

MAKKA: Volkov is here, Papotchka. VOLKOV.

KALASHNIKOV: Volkov, Volkov.
    I told you, I never knew any 'Volkov'.

MAKKA: His father then. Worked with you. For you. Against
    you, back in the day, how do I know?

*She sighs, exasperated.*

MAKKA: You do this on purpose. Don't think I don't notice,
    Papa.

KALASHNIKOV: Say again?

MAKKA: You hear what you want to hear.

KALASHNIKOV: *(Out.)* Don't listen.

MAKKA: It must be a visitor, he's been driving around the lake edge like a drunkard. You've got him lost, papa. You are rotten.

KALASHNIKOV: He must have money – a taxi this far.

MAKKA: Not poor anyway – I said, he's from Moscow. You're not going to meet him dressed like that?

*KALASHNIKOV slaps the back of his neck – a mosquito.*

KALASHNIKOV: In the summer the bugs around our lake grow big as bulldozers.

*He looks at the tiny corpse, then back up at the sky.*

KALASHNIKOV: Not even spring yet. One of the advance party.

MAKKA: Papa.

KALASHNIKOV: Still cold, at first light. We had to keep moving, Elena and I, in the woods.

MAKKA: PAPA – WHAT WILL YOU DO ABOUT VOLKOV?

KALASHNIKOV: IF YOU SHOUT THERE'S NO POINT ME WEARING IT.

*MAKKA bites back her exasperation, and finds a patient tone.*

MAKKA: Well...?

*Now she's got his attention. Beat. He sniffs – a characteristic twitch.*

KALASHNIKOV: Let him come. Let him explore the beauty of Udmurtia.

MAKKA: You should have told him how to find us properly. You don't behave well with people.

KALASHNIKOV: What should I do, light fires?

MAKKA: Be polite. He sounded…interested, on the phone. Respectful.

KALASHNIKOV: Respect. Thanks to my success as an engineer Makka has enjoyed a sheltered life.
If the journalist son of Nikolai Volkov has any 'respect' he'll find his own way. Nobody pulled up any trees for Kalashnikov, that I can tell you.

MAKKA: So you do know him. You knew his father.

*Beat. KALASHNIKOV takes a gadget and screwdriver from his dressing gown pocket.*

KALASHNIKOV: *(Out.)* Retired, that's my official position. Nobody retires these days, do they.

MAKKA: Papa. Change? Please?

KALASHNIKOV: *(A title.)* Misha Kalashnikov develops the prototype of an important new device.
A suit won't help.

*Beat.*

MAKKA: Well of course, if it's work. Put a jacket on at least.

*She is back to her washing. Again, KALASHNIKOV gives in. He puts the gadget aside, opens the door of the tool store and swaps his dressing gown for a marginally less scruffy combat jacket, hanging on the back of the door. Underneath he is wearing an old t-shirt and saggy jogging pants.*

MAKKA: Elena's clothes were filthy. What time were you out this morning?

KALASHNIKOV: *(Smiling.)* Up before the birds. She's out there now, organizing the defences.

MAKKA: She's too young to be left alone.

KALASHNIKOV: I'll find her. Getting hard though. She's like a fairy, knows the forest like the back of her hand.

MAKKA: She's twelve years old, Papa, a child.

KALASHNIKOV: She defeated Hitler this morning! The Nazis pinned us down, but Elena, she led the counter – she has courage that one!
A proper Russian fairy.

MAKKA: She's put a spell on you, alright.

KALASHNIKOV: What can I say? My children produced nicer offspring than I did.
If only we'd come up with an AK42. We'd have beaten the Nazis from day one. Stalingrad would have been over in a week. Tops.

*Off, noise of a car engine, another mosquito, drawing closer now. They stop to listen. Then MAKKA puts down the basket, straightens herself, takes a step toward the house, as if to take action – perhaps attract the car – but her father dissuades her.*

KALASHNIKOV: Leave it. I need to get my thoughts together.
*(Commanding.)* Makka!

*A beat. There's no mistaking the steel in KALASHNIKOV's voice. MAKKA gives in. They stand listening. The engine tails off, getting more distant, and then the car is gone.*

MAKKA: There. Happy now?

*He spreads his arms, showing off the jacket.*

KALASHNIKOV: Happy now?

*Beat.*

MAKKA: The noise before. The squealing. When I came out here, you said The beasts.

KALASHNIKOV: That was nothing.

MAKKA: Papa…!

KALASHNIKOV: I was younger than Elena!
>  They slaughtered the livestock. Ours and all the
>  kulaks'.

MAKKA: It's history, Papa…

KALASHNIKOV: Great crowd of men, out of the blue. Herded
>  all the cows, bulls, ewes, into the yard – slitting throats.
>  The most hideous noise you ever heard. Beast after
>  beast, pitiless. You couldn't cross the yard, for grease.
>  My Papa was a hard man – never mind 'Kulak', there
>  was a peasant's peasant. 'Misha – cover the blood with
>  snow, there's a good lad'. I fetched more snow, more
>  and more, carted it round from the neighbour's yard in
>  a wheelbarrow. Snow on snow, piling it up. Hopeless.
>  On the up side, that was the day I learned a man could
>  fell a great big bull with one blow of an axe, if he
>  picked his spot.
>  Ker-pow!
>  Eleven years of age? I was impressed. Fantastic!
>  They shipped us all off after that – all the kulaks – in of
>  all things, cattle trucks. Ha!

MAKKA: *(Gently.)* Papotchka. Maybe you should see a doctor.

*He is having trouble with the hearing aid again.*

MAKKA: YOU SHOULD SEE A DOCTOR.

KALASHNIKOV: I SAW A DOCTOR.

MAKKA: AND?

KALASHNIKOV: It proved the eyes are working.

MAKKA: And the noise?

KALASHNIKOV: Rejoice. I'm not deaf to everything.
>  You heard them too, Makka – maybe you should see a
>  doctor.
>  *(Out.)* Maybe you should all see a doctor.

*She is weary at his evasion. He sits, wearily.*

KALASHNIKOV: When you get to my age, you're like a child: anything that works is a source of wonder.

I dreamed last night I was a colander under a tap. I could feel myself full of holes, water gushing, every pore – wooosh. I woke up, I thought, You've wet the bed you old fool. I hadn't – sheets, dry as a bone. I beat myself up all night for no reason.

MAKKA: Whatever happens Papotchka… It's just one interview. Nothing bad can happen. I won't let it. It's good for us.

*MAKKA kisses his head affectionately, he softens.*

KALASHNIKOV: Makka, Makka Makka, my second-best daughter. Where would I be without you.

MAKKA: Exactly where you are – in that terrible jacket.

*KALASHNIKOV's turn to be exasperated – he can't win. MAKKA exits to the dacha with the washing basket.*

*Left alone, KALASHNIKOV starts to sing. A folk song about snow…*

Under white snow the blustery night covered the path along which you and I walked together, my dear. Beloved, remember our meetings, and the words of love you spoke to me. Why did you forget those moments, those hours we spent together? I suffered, I waited. I waited, and I called to you in sadness. But the path only got buried more and more, and the familiar tracks disappeared far away.*

*The song trails away… He speaks to himself/us.*

KALASHNIKOV: 'De-kulakisation' Not easy, disposing of a whole class – even in a country this big.

(*Calling.*) Say what you like Makka, Russia achieved things in those days.

* Please see Appendix for song lyrics (page 82)

*Offstage, the buzz of an intercom, and a voice, calling.*

(VOLKOV): Hullo?! Anyone home…? Hullo?

KALASHNIKOV: O Bugger. Makka…Makka! Don't let him in, for godsake…

*VOLKOV appears, eyes only, in the sky. It is revealed as a screen.*

*Film/Live Feed:*

VOLKOV: Hello… Hello?

*He stands back from the camera…we see a parka-clad man, with a grip bag by his feet. Behind him is the road. He smoothes his hair as he waits.*

VOLKOV: Hello?

MAKKA: *(Off, calling.)* Hello??

*We hear MAKKA fumble with the intercom, then speak into it, her efficient voice.*

MAKKA: *(Off.)* Yes, who is it? Name please.

KALASHNIKOV: *(Protesting.)* Makka…!

*On the 'screen' VOLKOV steps forward again – close-up of his face.*

VOLKOV: Hello? It's Volkov. From Gazettia? I have an appointment with General Kalashnikov. This is the Kalashnikov residence?... Hello?

MAKKA: *(Off.)* Gate's open. Enter.

*The sound of a buzzer, and an automated gate clangs open. We might glimpse it as VOLKOV steps back.*

VOLKOV: Thank you.

*VOLKOV steps forward. Sky returns to its normal blank state.*

*KALASHNIKOV, exasperated, throws down the gadget he has been fiddling with.*

KALASHNIKOV: Bugger.

*A moment later, VOLKOV has appeared stage right, as from the road, the bag slung over his shoulder, snow on his boots. On seeing the old man, he is awestruck.*

VOLKOV: Is it you, General? General Mikhail Timofeyevich Kalashnikov...?!

*Beat. KALASHNIKOV sniffs.*

KALASHNIKOV: Who's asking.

VOLKOV: Volkov. From Gazettia. Please, Dmitry – Dmitry Nikolaevich Volkov. My father was Nikolai Volkov – obviously. From St Petersburg? Petrograd. I work for Gazettia Film now, in Moscow. The journalist. You've been expecting me...?

*Beat.*

KALASHNIKOV: Speak up. I'm deaf.

*Enter MAKKA, being cool.*

MAKKA: Ah, you found us ok then, Volkov.

VOLKOV: No. Not at all.

*VOLKOV enters more fully into the space, dropping his bag, removing gloves.*

VOLKOV: I've been driving like a drunkard along the lake edge. The General's directions were faultless of course. My mistake. Several mistakes. I am...I parked down the road a little – the end of a track, a track going nowhere. Ditch, in fact... No matter.

KALASHNIKOV: *(Puzzled)* You drove to Udmurtia...?

VOLKOV: From the airport. A hire car, very new. *Was...*(very new.)

MAKKA: From the airport, Papa. Volkov's from Moscow.

*Beat. KALASHNIKOV sniffs, unimpressed.*

VOLKOV: Perhaps I might borrow a shovel later?
Perhaps a rope...?

MAKKA: Manners, Papa, you see?
And a good jacket.

*KALASHNIKOV sniffs, sets about finding a bottle, glasses.*

MAKKA: I should warn you Volkov. Papa can be difficult,
when he's working.

*VOLKOV attempts to shake hands with his quarry.*

VOLKOV: It's a privilege to meet you, General.

*KALASHNIKOV proffers the glasses.*

KALASHNIKOV: Drink, comrade?

*He sets about pouring the drinks.*

VOLKOV: I...I have just a few questions. You know the reason
for my visit...?

MAKKA: A short film. A series Volkov's making...

KALASHNIKOV: A series now?

VOLKOV: Interviews with Stalin's children. We plan to call it,
'Great inventors of the past'.

*Beat.*

KALASHNIKOV: But you'll have a glass first, surely?

*VOLKOV assents, weakly, to the already poured drink.*

VOLKOV: It's a lovely dacha you have, General.

KALASHNIKOV: Modest the house, but fair the view.

VOLKOV: *(Looking about.)* Forest. Very dark forest.

KALASHNIKOV: The lake. And Izhmash, the most beautiful
motor factory in all the Russias.

*KALASHNIKOV toasts the factory. VOLKOV raises his glass but moves on before drinking.*

VOLKOV: I thought we might start at the beginning.
      The childhood years.

*He reins himself in.*

VOLKOV: The General's childhood's not widely known. A
      good start, I thought.

*He is appealing to MAKKA for support. KALASHNIKOV sniffs.*

KALASHNIKOV: A terrible start. We'll move on.
      I've laid out the parts of my life. There are no secrets.

*He is referring to the gun. VOLKOV sees the parts.*

VOLKOV: You want to begin with the gun.

KALASHNIKOV: AK-47, be all and end all. There's the gesture
      of a life in that rifle, comrade. A life's work in eight
      parts.
      Drink up.

MAKKA: Papa, perhaps Volkov doesn't want to drink. Work
      first, drink later? At ten in the morning. I'll bring some
      coffee.

*MAKKA exits to the house.*

KALASHNIKOV: Makka – my second best daughter. My eyes,
      my ears. Also my conscience.

VOLKOV: Enchanting.

KALASHNIKOV: She has a daughter of her own, somewhere.
      A fairy, spying on us. Elena knows this forest like the
      back of her hand. Ruthless with invaders.

VOLKOV: A daughter? What a coincidence. I have a
      daughter myself.
      People always seem surprised. We have great hopes for
      her. Angelina takes piano lessons in St Petersburg.

KALASHNIKOV: Elena doesn't care for strangers. Move
    suddenly and she'll open up with artillery.

*Beat.*

VOLKOV: But you must see many strangers General, passing
    through. A man as famous as yourself.

KALASHNIKOV: Manufacturers, inventors, business types. The
    occasional president.
    *They* mostly just want a photograph. Or to pin
    something new on me. Journalists are no different.

VOLKOV: I imagine you must get quite a few from my
    profession, seeking you out.

KALASHNIKOV: I discourage them.

VOLKOV: But you agreed to our interview. When my producer
    called he spoke to your secretary, she distinctly said…

KALASHNIKOV: That would be Makka. Makka reads
    magazines. 'Marketing – the oxygen of commerce'.
    'The future of Russia lies with Europe'. 'Why
    talking is good for you'. I'll make a poor subject
    for interview. I've no religion, no guilt. I'm like a
    good toolbox – everything in its place, no spanners
    with the micrometers, no T-squares with the planes.
    If it's scandal you're after, you'll not find it here.
    Journalists? *(He scoffs.)*, traipsing to the door with their
    cameras and their puffa jackets…
    Where's your camera from, comrade?

*KALASHNIKOV looks closely at it. VOLKOV hasn't a clue where it's
made.*

VOLKOV: A hire service in Moscow. Japanese, I think.

KALASHNIKOV: Chinese manufacture.

VOLKOV: You disapprove?

KALASHNIKOV: Of the Chinese? Not particularly.

VOLKOV: But in general?

*Beat. Perhaps KALASHNIKOV has underestimated this city boy.*

KALASHNIKOV: The Chinese are copyists. Most of the AKs in the world are theirs – millions of them, a stack as long as the wall of China, made on licence. No licence I ever granted.

VOLKOV: But they…what? They pay a royalty, surely?

KALASHNIKOV: The Soviet world was always generous with technology. I never made a penny from arms sales. You can record that Volkov. Do it now, in fact. If you don't mind. A condition of my participation.

VOLKOV: Well I'm not really…(ready yet).

KALASHNIKOV: I'll wait.

*Pause. VOLKOV prepares the camera and mic, makes sure the camera is switched on, then repeats his (slightly re-formulated) question.*

VOLKOV: General Kalashnikov – am I correct in believing the Chinese do not pay a royalty for their copies of the AK47?

KALASHNIKOV: I personally never made a penny from arms sales, from AK47s made in Russia or China. Or Bulgaria, Hungary, Romania, Poland, India, Pakistan, Indonesia, or Vietnam. Or Egypt. Or Israel. Or would you believe, the United States of America. Nothing from any of the AKs made anywhere in the world ever entered my pocket. My work was a gift to the Motherland. For which I was paid a worker's wage, and that's fine.
You can stop now.

*VOLKOV does so.*

VOLKOV: General Kalashnikov, it's a very great honour to meet you. I must tell you, my father was a huge admirer. He passed away last year.

KALASHNIKOV: O, I'm sorry.

VOLKOV: My producer thought, since we had such strong familial connections…

KALASHNIKOV: Familial connections?

VOLKOV: Brothers in arms. My father and yourself, young Soviet engineers together.

My film will show the winds of fortune, how paths diverge – General Kalashnikov achieving great things in the field of engineering – with the help of market forces, going on to achieve much recognition in the world. My father, by contrast… *not* going on. We will show how he, through adversity, became a lesser figure. Dwindled, lost hope. A casualty, caught in the wheels of a relentless, pitiless machine.

KALASHNIKOV: We're all equal under the flag, comrade.

*MAKKA enters with a coffee pot.*

KALASHNIKOV: I should be clear about this, Volkov…

VOLKOV: Dmitry Nikolaevich. Please.

KALASHNIKOV: I should tell you, Volkov, whatever Makka said, whatever she promised, whatever you're hoping, I don't remember your father. Nothing.

MAKKA: *(Chiding.)* Papa…!

VOLKOV: But you must. Forgive me General – the Polygon in Moscow, the development team there. My father was in Simonov's team. Volkov the engineer. You and he met at mealtimes. Talked, sometimes…discussing the problems of new weapons – the calibration of ammunition, the problems of recoil, and…and so on. Papa treasured those days – his days as an engineer… He often spoke of his great comrade Kalashnikov. The one true genius of his field.

KALASHNIKOV: Is that right.

MAKKA: You see Papa, you're an inspiration. Even today in modern...

KALASHNIKOV: *(Anticipating.)*...in modern Russia.

*KALASHNIKOV sniffs.*

KALASHNIKOV: You've got a mark on your nose, Makka just there.

*Beat. Chastened, MAKKA finishes setting/clearing pots, and exits. When she's gone...*

KALASHNIKOV: An interview, Dmitry Nikolaevich.

VOLKOV: An interview. Very brief.

*Beat. KALASHNIKOV gives way.*

VOLKOV: Now?

KALASHNIKOV: One of our great slogans, 'The future is ours'. When a man, when a society, is as close to the end as this, we live only in the present.

VOLKOV: Providing one can ignore the past.
You've lived a long life, General. Let's hope we have enough film.

KALASHNIKOV: Your camera's digital, comrade. There's no film.

*Beat. It's clear KALASHNIKOV does not intend to be patronised.*

VOLKOV: Of course.
Perhaps, then, we might begin with 'Exile'.
To modern Russians there is a fascinating paradox here; a young boy's family is exiled, expelled by Stalin – yet this same boy becomes devoted to the Soviet system. That is a perplexing reaction to many modern minds.

KALASHNIKOV: This will be part two then.

VOLKOV: Sorry?

KALASHNIKOV: A life in eight parts. Part One; Slaughter of the Beasts. You missed that. Part Two; the Old Believers.

2

VOLKOV: Part Two. The Old...?

KALASHNIKOV: The Old Believers.

*The camera is on. Both are slightly more self-conscious now.*

VOLKOV: You were religious, then General, as a family? The Old Believers.

KALASHNIKOV: Mother was a religious woman. We children said our prayers, or appeared to.

VOLKOV: You were never a believer yourself?

KALASHNIKOV: Never.
Religion is the opiate of the people.

*VOLKOV stops the camera.*

VOLKOV: General Kalashnikov is being humorous.

KALASHNIKOV: No.

*Beat. VOLKOV restarts the camera.*

VOLKOV: So the Old Believers. This is a reference to your parents' religion...?

KALASHNIKOV: No. My mother was never of that sect. She was devoted to the Orthodox religion. Then we arrived in Niznhe-Mokhavaya...

VOLKOV: Where you were brutally exiled by Stalin...

KALASHNIKOV: Where we were exiled, in Siberia. A territory crammed with victims of purges past. Pity these holy Old Believers. Four hundred years of exile in that godforsaken land, believing themselves the elect. Then the Kulaks turn up, tipped out of our cattle trucks like

41

rotten teeth. The Old Believers were ordered to give rooms of their houses over to us. A cruel lesson for pious people, don't you think – till then persecution was proof of holiness.

VOLKOV: Naturally they disapproved of you – of your mother's religion, your own lack of it?

KALASHNIKOV: Their panic seemed religious. In fact, it was more a matter of vegetables.

*A dumbfounded pause.*

KALASHNIKOV: Shall I go on?

*VOLKOV clears his throat.*

VOLKOV: Perhaps you could expand on that thought for us General. Vegetables?

*KAKASHNIKOV addresses the camera directly – this might be seen on screens.*

KALASHNIKOV: Who of you ever tried peeing in a bucket on a moving train? Try shitting in a bucket in the same circumstance! Packed into wagons like sardines in a can, hot in the day, freezing at night, begging food from passers-by when we passed through a station. When the train finally stopped, we walked for a week skirting around marshes, a feast for mosquitoes. By the time we arrived in Niznhe-Mokhavaya I for one was in a terrible condition. Like one of those horsemen of the apocalypse, Pestilence probably. These Old Believers thought the end of their world had come – thought we'd fall on their spuds, wreak utter desolation.

VOLKOV: And were you reduced to that, General? To thieving from the starving, to survive the exile Stalin forced upon you?

KALASHNIKOV: My father was a hard man – a peasant's peasant. We've not suffered the winters they've suffered in this place, he said, Make allowances lads.

He was right. We hadn't begun to suffer. Not then.

VOLKOV: So, you admired them for their survival. These Old
Believers.

*Beat.*

KALASHNIKOV: I thought they were fools. The whole country
was transforming! I made my mind up never to bring
suffering on myself by believing anything so against the
flow of history.
The historical inevitability of socialism – that's what
impressed me. So much change in so short a time –
compare that with four hundred years of praying. They
gained nothing but starvation.

VOLKOV: This then, was when you first became a true
socialist. A comrade.

KALASHNIKOV: This was when I decided to do everything in
my power to rejoin the revolution. The first thing they
told us when we arrived in Siberia? You are enemies
of the people, *vrag naroda* – you've lost the right to call
anyone comrade. Forever.
Like an iceberg, drifting in an endless sea.
How I became a citizen is a longer story. Not very
noble. Though it did involve a gun.
We'll stop there shall we.

VOLKOV: General, this sounds interesting. You say…

KALASHNIKOV: Please. If you don't mind, Volkov.

*Again, the steel in KALASHNIKOV is unmistakeable. VOLKOV
obliges.*

KALASHNIKOV: This engineer – this Volkov – he taught you
weapons I take it?

VOLKOV: My father… Nikolai Illyich was not a believer in
arms, in later life.

KALASHNIKOV: Pity. Do you know what this is?

*He has picked up one of the components.*

VOLKOV: I should, I know…

KALASHNIKOV: *(Out.)* Anyone?
Comrades, you've not paid attention. This is part three.

3

*Enter MAKKA – she has changed, fixed her hair, put on a little make-up – and some self-consciousness.*

MAKKA: So, you made a start, that's good.

VOLKOV: Yes. We're already at part three, apparently. Your father is a natural, in front of the camera.

MAKKA: He'll be glossing over things. DON'T GLOSS THINGS OVER PAPA. It's not fair.
He's told you about his father?

VOLKOV: Yes, declared a kulak, an enemy of the people.

MAKKA: He died, the first winter in Siberia. Did Papa tell you his body lay dead in the house for a week? The ground outside too hard, too frozen for his little sons to bury him.

KALASHNIKOV: Makka, that's enough.…

MAKKA: Revolution's a lovely thing close up, don't you think, Volkov? All his life Papa kept his past a secret – even I knew nothing about his suffering, not for years.

KALASHNIKOV: Plenty of people suffered back then. There was nothing special about us.

MAKKA: You mean you can't make a new world without breaking a few heads?

KALASHNIKOV: If that's how you want it. Maybe.
Was it necessary? Who knows. But I came out of that time determined to serve my country. I didn't waste the

44

life I was given, I haven't lived it selfishly. How many people can say that?

MAKKA: *(Gentle but firm.)* Papa. You weren't given a life by the soviets. You took it.

KALASHNIKOV: Ha! It's true my comrades were slow to recognise a patriot.

*(To MAKKA.)* Wait – I haven't finished with you.

Makka's right, there are some things should not be glossed over. The first time I ever held a gun in my hands, was the first time I tried to become a citizen.

Part Number Three; Guns and their uses.

Camera rolling. Stand over there. Makka please. Please.

The camera is on. Kalashnikov has picked up the AK's stock – pretty much the skeleton of the rifle. He refers to the camera.

KALASHNIKOV: Is it running?

Imagine this is a rifle, an old hunting gun – belonged to a friend of mine, Gavril.

When father died, mother married a neighbour. It was no place for a woman to be without protection, and he was a decent enough type. A few years passed and it dawned on Gavril and me we'd survived. It was time to get out of this nowhere place, rejoin our society, become patriots, but without passports it was impossible. For passports, documents were required – we were *Vrag naroda*. That's when I made my first proper invention – a stamp to seal documents I forged myself. The plan was to walk 800 kilometres back to Kurya, present our documents, get a passport, begin our new life. 800 kilometres on foot, passing through every village checkpoint, all with orders to shoot anyone who might be an imperialist spy. All the tools we had were my forged papers, and this old hunting rifle Gavril got hold of. One rifle between two youths – he was a bit older than me. How did we do it? Volkov?

VOLKOV: I…have no idea. Train?

KALASHNIKOV: The trains were watched, ditches were filling
up with spies.
Makka?
Anyone?

*He levels the gun at VOLKOV.*

KALASHNIKOV: Hands up!

MAKKA: Papa!!

KALASHNIKOV: You too!!
Step away from the house. Now back. You see?
Prisoner and guard – Gavril was the guard, I was his
prisoner. Never failed.
Well eventually it failed. Somebody looked too closely
at the stamp, found a flaw in my work. An important
lesson for an inventor. No matter how good an
invention is, you can always, always, make it better. Too
late for Gavril and me, our game was up.
Kalashnikov puts the rifle stock down, while Volkov
tries to keep the ball rolling.

VOLKOV: So, what – you fired the gun?

KALASHNIKOV: Ha! I'd dismantled our rifle a thousand
times, every night in the forest, lying low, learning the
principles of its construction. It was clear it would never
fire. We did the only practical thing we could think of;
ran for our lives. Dashed into the woods, a part buried
here, a piece thrown there – scattered, all through the
forest. Get caught with a weapon in private possession,
that would be a disaster. Finally the villagers gave up
the chase. We were free. Free to go back, try again the
next year, succeed in the end. So. An old gun, together,
scattered, shaped my life. And my life shaped the
AK47.
Guns, are practical you see. Or should be. Designing
them means overcoming a never-ending series of

problems. Solve a complex problem in a simple way! In the words of my design hero Shpagin, Complexity's easy – it's simplicity that's hard. That's what my life has been about, the practical concerns of an engineer. Nothing more. A whole lifetime.

Now if you'll excuse me, somewhere in the woods I have a granddaughter waiting to be attacked. We can talk later Volkov, if you're here. Makka will look after you.

*Exit KALASHNIKOV, to the woods. Pause, during which VOLKOV turns off the camera.*

VOLKOV: A remarkable man.

MAKKA: Yes. You must forgive him, Volkov.

VOLKOV: There's nothing to forgive.

Not for me to forgive, anyway.

MAKKA: Talking too much. Or too little.

We must all be kind to Papa now. You probably guessed, Dmitry Nikolaevich. My father's dying.

*Lights fade.*

4

*The side of the toolstore becomes a screen.*

*Film: ELENA is seen, sitting deep in the forest. She holds a number four – drawn on a scrap of cardboard – up to the camera. Underneath is the legend, 'The Great Patriotic War'. ELENA turns the cardboard over and draws on the other side while talking to us.*

ELENA: What my Granddad did in the war was drive a tank and invent things. He was smart, like me.

When he was a kid he invented loads of things for the farm, or the kitchen, so when he joined the army, he did the same. He made a machine for counting how many bullets his tank had fired, stuff like that – that's how he got to be called an inventor. Then he got shot

47

up by the Nazis and had to go to hospital. That was
so boring; weeks and weeks stuck in bed. All he could
do was read books about weapon design, and listen to
other men talking about how rubbish their guns were
– always jamming up or firing off-target. 'Aim for the
head comrade, shoot yourself in the foot'. That's when
he decided to invent a new gun, one with not so many
pieces you could lose. A gun you could drag through
mud or water, or get covered in snow, and still have a
weapon you could trust. Granddad beat loads of really
brainy people with his invention, in a competition for
the whole Russian army. *(Shrugs.)* Just because you
haven't been to school much isn't an excuse. Being
stupid wasn't an option. He won that competition and
his gun was called the AK-47. It was given to every
Russian soldier, even though it was too late for the
Patriotic war, against the Nazis. Granddad's gun helped
Russia fight the next war, the Cold War, and that's how
our family got to be famous.

*She holds the card up again. Now it has a big number five, and
'Uncle Joe's lake' written on it in ELENA's script.*


5

*Lights up on the same scene as before – later the same day, though the
garden is now in less than bright sunshine. A samovar has appeared
on the table.*

*MAKKA appears with plates, wiping them off with a cloth, and putting
them on the table.*

*As she does so, she speaks to someone offstage.*

MAKKA: Come and have tea.

*Waving, and calling upstage.*

MAKKA: Tea!

*VOLKOV enters from the direction of the jetty/lake. He carries
KALASHNIKOV's small metal contraption in his hand.*

VOLKOV: You're very brave, Mdm Kalashnikova.

MAKKA: Making tea? I don't think so.

VOLKOV: Eating outdoors, this time of year.

MAKKA: O, this isn't cold. Not for Udmurtia. Have a chair.

VOLKOV: *(Pressing his point.)* There's a man out there cutting a fishing-hole in the ice!
At least I think it was a man. Are there bears in these woods?

MAKKA: Lots. Papa keeps saying he's going to bag one, but he hasn't shot one yet.
*(Looking to the lake.)* Brave, whoever it is, this close to spring. The ice melts.
They do breed people tough round here. Inbreed.

*Beat.*

MAKKA: Tea?

VOLKOV: Yes, thank you.

MAKKA: *(As she exits to the house.)* Help yourself. I'll bring food.

VOLKOV: I'm quite afraid of bears.

*He looks back at the contraption in his hands, then puts it on the table and pours his tea from the samovar, MAKKA returns, carrying a casserole.*

VOLKOV: It's a remarkable thing you're doing, living here, looking after the General.

MAKKA: No, not remarkable – we only came for the summer.
Then Papa got ill, I took time off. I'm a teacher really, in Perm. We did try Elena in the local school, but…
That was not a good fit.
*(Brightly.)* Now I have my own class again.

VOLKOV: A class of one.

MAKKA: Ah, but what a one. She's in her element now, my
Elena. More a goblin than a fairy these days, whatever
Papa says.

VOLKOV: She must miss her friends, though. And you, your
colleagues…?

MAKKA: I suppose. The children round here are as bad as the
parents. They made Elena's life a misery. *(Brightly.)* It's
much cheaper living out here, and now she's happy.
Not many girls Elena's age can spot the difference
between forged and pressed steel. Not many have an
exhaustive knowledge of ballistics. There's stew, if
you're hungry – elk. Papa makes the stock himself.
Hunt the beast, skin the beast, boil the bones.

VOLKOV: O. So, perhaps he's the goblin.
Mmmm – smells good. You're not eating yourself,
Makka Mikhailovna?

*She waves her hand – she prefers to smoke.*

VOLKOV: You don't seem very concerned about Elena, your
father.

MAKKA: Oh.
I haven't told her yet. Elena's father died when she was
six. It doesn't seem fair.

VOLKOV: I meant, are they normally out this long?

MAKKA: Oh – whole days, sometimes. I'm starting to think
Papa's right – a few weeks in the forest and her life
will be surging like a spring. Believe me, Dmitry
Nikolaevich, Elena knows these woods like the…

VOLKOV: …like the back of her hand. Just what the General
said.

MAKKA: There you are. We agree.
Papa was always working when I was her age. She's
having the childhood I never had.

    I am sorry, Dmitry Nikolaevich, you're worried about your interview.

VOLKOV: Ah. Dmitry, please.

MAKKA: Dmitry. Then you must call me Makka.

VOLKOV: Makka.

*Beat.*

MAKKA: What? Something on my face again?

VOLKOV: No no, I was trying to picture you…(as a child). Forgive me, it's a thing I do. Picturing people when they were young.

*Beat.*

VOLKOV: As a child, I mean.

MAKKA: *(Recovering.)* What age were you thinking of?

VOLKOV: Oh… How old is Elena now? Twelve, you say?

MAKKA: Yes. Alright, eyes closed. OK – I'm about so high – sorry. To about here, bigger than Elena, able to look after myself. Buck teeth, pig tails, blue check skirt, woollen pullover – my sisters and mine, both identical. Two pairs of shoes, school and best. That marked us out. Not rich – people weren't rich then, we didn't think about it – but not bad. Papa only got this place four years ago. He finally got money from some marketing thing. Golfing umbrellas, I think, Kalashnikov hunting knives – they sell them in the town. He's had nothing from arms sales. He's very clear about that.

VOLKOV: He did mention it.

MAKKA: That's how it was back then. People worked, got paid – on paper, anyway. All working for a better world. Everything Papa made belonged to the state. It's only now I say, Papa, if you had a rouble for every Kalashnikov sold, we'd be living in a palace.

VOLKOV: What does he say to that?

MAKKA: He quotes Vershynin. 'The socialist enters a palace seeking only a torch.'
That's what's odd about the Americans. Who knows who designed the M16? Who cares? But every American inventor is a millionaire. Papa, everyone knows what he invented – we get letters from everywhere, Australia, Moscow, he's never had a thing. I'm sorry I'm talking about money, I don't mean to. It's him.

VOLKOV: I feel protective about my father. Did.
Our parents lived through astonishing times, Makka Mikhailovna.

MAKKA: Yes.

*Beat.*

MAKKA: Bit younger I suppose, your parents…?

VOLKOV: Oh…(hardly).
My father was an engineer too.

MAKKA: Yes.

VOLKOV: Gifted, I think. Someone accused him of a misdemeanour. He was re-assigned to clerical work, hated every minute. We lived under a cloud when I was young.

MAKKA: Oh I'm sorry. That must have been hard.

VOLKOV: 'Our parents lived through astonishing times'.

*Beat.*

MAKKA: Papa talks about those days as if it was the lake. If you ask him, he'll sound nostalgic. It was simpler, I suppose. Everyone walked on thin ice then – your parents, mine, no choice. Everyone working out where the ice was thinnest, trying not to go near. Step on the wrong part in those days, you'd fall right through, disappear forever.

VOLKOV: As many people did.

*Beat.*

MAKKA: Your father was lucky, really, Dmitry Nikolaevich. He wasn't sent to the gulag, or into exile. Cruel, I'm sorry that sounds so…

VOLKOV: No no. You're right of course. We were lucky. We survived.

MAKKA: Nothing astonishing today. Everyone lost in the tangle of the new Russia.

VOLKOV: Really…?

MAKKA: I think so. The whole of life is a forest now – except there are no big beasts to follow. Paths made by no more than a rabbit or a deer. We follow what we think might be a path, hope it leads somewhere. Papa was lucky – he walked on thin ice for years and years; for years and years he had to be so careful. It never cracked.
Forest, ice – as you can see, Dmitry Nikolaevitch; I teach poetry.

*They laugh. Pause. VOLKOV presses on, carefully.*

VOLKOV: He did join the Party, though, Kalashnikov. That wasn't exactly thin ice, was it…?

MAKKA: Papa was *Vrag naroda*. He kept his head down for years, worked hard and he was successful. Then one day they decide to give him the Lenin medal. Suddenly he has to get hold of a Party card, has to fill in the application form.

VOLKOV: So they did find out? About his origins.

MAKKA: No. Probably they knew. Probably it was on file
somewhere – in case he went off the rails. They were
very good at that kind of thing, as you know.

VOLKOV: He didn't ever…(go off the rails?)

MAKKA: Papa? No, too busy working.

*Beat.*

There was a woman in Irkutsk, I think.

VOLKOV: Really?

MAKKA: Women throw themselves at you, when you're a
Hero. Papa always came home to Mama though, kept
working. Working for us and for the Motherland.
You can put that in your film: the AK-47 didn't just save
Russia, it saved Papa. Saved all of us. We had no idea
he was in danger.
Did you know what had happened to your father – at
the time?

VOLKOV: No, no. An atmosphere.
And your sister, the matching pullover? – the General
called you his second best daughter.

MAKKA: Oh that.
We lost Nonna in an accident. A car crash – a few years
ago now.

VOLKOV: I'm sorry.

MAKKA: It was Nonna looked after Papa when Mama died. I'd
got away by then. Papa never forgot.

Volkov: You're here now though, you've brought Elena into
his life.

MAKKA: Yes. Perhaps you're right, my star is rising. Up till
now it's just been Elena and I, mostly.

*Beat.*

Did you work that thing out yet?

VOLKOV: Oh…this? No. A very clever sprung mechanism…

*He has picked up the contraption again.*

MAKKA: Papa's inventions, they just flow out of him. You know, even though he was a Hero, we still had to take whatever house the Party gave us. Give it up too, if they told us, which they did, more than once.

VOLKOV: They took your house away?

MAKKA: O, not this one. We lived in town first, the tiniest apartment. We had to move overnight. You should picture me very young with a parcel of cabbage under my arm. That was winter, real winter. There was snow on Papa's gloves, great flakes of it in the night. Ice really. Cabbage under one arm, my hand in his glove, big ice flakes, trudging along the street. I remember feeling very safe, and alive.

*Pause.*

MAKKA: What kind of house do you have? You and your wife. Do you live in Moscow itself or…(outside?)

VOLKOV: Ah – no wife. Now. I have a room near the office. Not quite the gulag, but...

MAKKA: Better than here. Hard not to hate this place some days.

VOLKOV: And today, Makka Mikhailovna? Is your life surging like a spring?

*MAKKA smiles.*

MAKKA: Today, it's nice.

*He smiles. She smiles. The mole trap – for that's what it is – snaps on VOLKOV's fingers. He is on his feet, in anguish.*

VOLKOV: Aaaagh!

MAKKA: Oh no! I'm sorry, I should have warned you!

VOLKOV: It's a gintrap!!!

MAKKA: No no a mole catcher! Oh god – a prototype. I'm so sorry!..

VOLKOV: Aaagh, no, it's fine… If I can just…aggh aggh…

*He prizes it open and extracts his fingers…*

MAKKA: I'll get a bandage…

VOLKOV: No no…really, I'll be…it's fine… It's…
…efficient…

MAKKA: Of course, Papa's design…

*They laugh.*

MAKKA: I'll fetch a cold compress…

VOLKOV: No no please. Makka. It's fine…

MAKKA: You're sure…? It's no trouble...

VOLKOV: No No, please. I'd like to ask you a question. If I may.

*Beat.*

MAKKA: Alright.

VOLKOV: The General – your father – he wasn't just a Party member. Later. He was a member of the Supreme Soviet, for quite a time…?

*Beat. MAKKA is exasperated or disappointed, or both. She very deliberately stubs out her cigarette.*

VOLKOV: Ah, now I've upset you.

MAKKA: I just…I hoped you would honour a Russian Hero. Not attack a sick old man.

VOLKOV: But I...I have to research his life, Makka
Mikhailovna...Is the Soviet something he's ashamed
of...?

MAKKA: Why can't people understand? The Supreme Soviet
was a rubber-stamping operation, for the Politburo.
Here, in Udmurtia, Papa had some power, some
influence – only the kind a shop steward has. Drove
Mama crazy: always someone in the kitchen at some
ridiculous hour begging to see the Representative. A
blocked access or a noisy neighbour, or a 'help get
our son into the best technical college'. Papa helped a
great many people in Izhevsk. This is a town – a city,
supposedly – that barely had a mile of tarmac till Papa
became deputy. But you live in Moscow, if there's one
thing you're not short of it's...success.

VOLKOV: But your father did believe he was working for
Stalin.

MAKKA: No. Stalin worked for Russia, Papa worked for Russia
too. They were...co-workers. Comrades.

VOLKOV: And Kalashnikov idolised Stalin. Does now. Even
after everything that we lived through, through those
astonishing times...

MAKKA: Not idolise.

*Beat.*

MAKKA: *(Brightly.)* I should tell you a story, Dmitry
Nikolaevitch.

VOLKOV: O...Can it hurt...?

MAKKA: Let me get you a compress, please...

VOLKOV: No no... See? I can straighten my fingers already,
almost. Prototype. I look forward to seeing the real
thing...

MAKKA: Papa's story. Stalin turns up at the Soviet two or three
times, when Papa is there. Three times at the most –
this particular time, the last time, all the deputies clap
when Comrade General Secretary comes in, obviously.
Papa claps too. They clap and clap, and still clap and
Papa glances from the corner of his eye, and he realises
how it is. A terrible game has begun. Who will dare be
the first to stop applauding Stalin? They'd still be there
now if the old…bastard hadn't lifted up his hand.

Papa would go mad if he heard me talk like that.

Papa was proud of Stalin, that generation are. They
were frightened, (but) they thought this is what the rest
of the world feels. To be invaded, to starve, to come
very close to being conquered – to realise the rest of
the world fears you, it felt good. That's how I think it
was, the Cold War, all of that. A time when Russia was
terrible and great.

He is consistent. I suppose consistency's still admirable.
Or is that being reactionary?

*Pause. VOLKOV tellingly doesn't respond.*

MAKKA: It's no joke then. Your title, 'Great inventors of
the past'. You plan to denounce Papa. Destroy his
reputation.

Are you even a journalist?

*MAKKA makes to exit, noisily picking up dishes. VOLKOV stands to
make a speech – he might flip on the camera and address it, recording
his credentials.*

VOLKOV: We salute General Mikhail Timofeyavich
Kalashnikov – a true Russian genius. My own father
said he would hold Kalashnikov's work in his hands
and be amazed – the simplicity. 'Kalashnikov will
never fix what isn't broken'. The revolving breach –
Kalashnikov invents it in 1946, it's used in every gun
the factory produces from then until now – why? It
works! Turns the bullet – just flying forward – it slots
so cleanly into the chamber – genius! The compressed

gasses, channelled back to force the next bullet home. Kalashnikov is always always trying to make a thing good, the best it can be. Kalashnikov believes in the common man, above all, he believes in the Russian soldier, in the Motherland.

*He turns off the camera. MAKKA hesitates.*

MAKKA: Well he was blown up in his tank.
Bound to give a man feeling for his comrades.

*They share a smile now.*

MAKKA: Sorry. I try to protect Papa. Since Nonna went back to god.
*(Mimic.)* Papa worked so hard, for what? she'd say. The whole of Russia turned into *alkashi*, hanging round the railway station!

*They smile again.*

MAKKA: He'll meet a bear when he does get back. I shall chew his head off. He's supposed to warn me if they're not coming to eat. That's why Papa loves it here; time means nothing.

VOLKOV: Should we save them some food, do you think?

MAKKA: No, no. Knowing Papa, they've killed, cooked and eaten something by now. They'll be out even longer.

*Beat.*

No good for your interview though. I am very sorry, Dmitry Nikolaevitch.

VOLKOV: That's fine, Makka Mikhailovna.

*He glances at his watch.*

MAKKA: City time – always flying.

VOLKOV: No no, there's no hurry, I'll just…

I shall have to interview the daughter of the General. About herself, this time.

*He puts camera back on.*

MAKKA: O, that won't take long...

VOLKOV: What age did we say? Twelve?

*VOLKOV closes his eyes, imagining. And opens them again.*

VOLKOV: Nope. I definitely prefer the woman Makka Mikhailovna is today. So...

*He gestures for MAKKA to sit before the camera.*

VOLKOV: What have you to say for yourself?

MAKKA: I told you. Nothing. What about you, I don't know anything about you. A good listener, you live in Moscow. How are things in Moscow? Is there plenty to buy in the shops? It always looks that way on TV.

VOLKOV: Oh plenty to buy – if you have money.

*A smile of recognition – they've returned to a familiar subject.*

VOLKOV: Last week there were bananas.

MAKKA: Yes I heard that, from America.

VOLKOV: Just seeing them somehow means you've not been forgotten. A gift between nations.

MAKKA: Better than exchanging missiles, I suppose.

*Smiles again, and a pause – a rather pregnant one.*

*Beat. MAKKA looks at the sky.*

MAKKA: You're right, it is still Winter out here.

*They smile. MAKKA suddenly kisses a non-plussed VOLKOV.*

MAKKA: Thank you, Dmitry. For helping me remember.

VOLKOV: Bananas?

MAKKA: Snow on Papa's gloves – ice. Being younger, feeling safe – feeling like a surging spring.

They'll be ages yet. I'm going to go inside. Get warm by the stove. I can show you Papa's study, if you like, you could do some filming there – if that would help…?

VOLKOV: Yes. Yes, that sounds very good, Makka Mik… (hailovna).

MAKKA: Good, Dmitry.

VOLKOV: *(Reciprocating.)* Makka.

*Beat. MAKKA gets up, makes to exit, VOLKOV picks up the mole trap on a stick or spoon.*

VOLKOV: I should probably…(put this somewhere…)

MAKKA: Sometimes, the best thing you can do in the woods is stop. Make a fire.

They'll be gone till dusk now.

I haven't felt the touch of anyone for a long time, Dmitry.

You?

VOLKOV: Yes. Yes, that's right.

*They are the only two people left in the world.*

MAKKA: We could finish the bottle, if you like.

*Beat. She exits to the house.*

*Pause. VOLKOV stays calm as he picks up the sketch pad, draws something, then props it on the table. It reads… '6: Ice and Fire'. He hesitates, and scribbles out the word 'Ice', and props it up again.*

*He picks up the bottle, and follows MAKKA into the house.*

*Long fade.*

## 6

*Film: Sky screen. Binoculars, in a snowy waste. They scan the sky. The breathing is heavy – it's very cold. We see the binoculars train on the dacha, and watch as the curtains in the dacha are pulled closed.*

*The binoculars are lowered and we see the watcher is ELENA. It's clear that she is neither surprised nor pleased by what she sees.*

*She determines to act: pulling down a ski mask to cover her face, she sets off.*

*Stealing into the garden of the dacha, and glancing towards the house to make sure she isn't seen, ELENA takes the camera and folds the tripod, sticking it all into VOLKOV's grip-bag – all achieved with great efficiency.*

*ELENA slings the bag onto her shoulder and is about to make off, when she stops: she has spotted the disassembled AK-47, lying where KALASHNIKOV left it in scene 2. Another, grander thought occurs to her: she carefully picks up the stock of the rifle…*

*'7: Into The Woods' appears on the screen, then screen fades.*

## 7

*Lights up on the garden, as before. Towards dusk. The table has not been cleared.*

*The camera has disappeared.*

*KALASHNIKOV emerges from the forest. He takes in the scene, including the mole trap, picks up a crust to chew on. He picks up the sketch book, glances at it and places it face down.*

*He lights a patio heater. It flares up, shedding some more light, which he augments by lighting other lamps. As he does so he begins to whistle, hum or sing, the same song as before.*

*When he's done that, he sits down – spoons some food onto a plate, and begins to eat.*

*VOLKOV enters from the dacha. He is nervous, seeing KALASHNIKOV.*

VOLKOV: General. We were almost giving up hope.

KALASHNIKOV: You didn't send out a search party then.

VOLKOV: Makka thought…Makka Mikhailovna and I, she imagined…
> Your daughter has great confidence in you, General, as a woodsman.

*KALASHNIKOV looks at him for the first time – and sniffs.*

KALASHNIKOV: (Is Makka) Inside?

*VOLKOV nods, and almost explains.*

VOLKOV: It's quite cold, out here.
> You're alright, both of you? Elena…?

*KALASHNIKOV pushes himself to his feet, wiping off his lips.*

KALASHNIKOV: Forgive me, Volkov. We should talk about your father.

VOLKOV: Yes, we were going to do that.

*VOLKOV glances at his watch.*

KALASHNIKOV: You'll stay the night? Now you've come this far?

VOLKOV: I should probably…(go).
> Yes. Thank you. I'll stay.

I can dig the car out any time.

*KALASHNIKOV goes to the tool shed and opens the door.*

KALASHNIKOV: Do you know what I keep in here?

VOLKOV: I should hope it's a shovel.

*KALASHNIKOV turns around, a bottle in his hand.*

VOLKOV: Ah.

KALASHNIKOV: Catch!

*KALASHNIKOV tosses the bottle over. Unnoticed by him, VOLKOV winces as he catches it.*

KALASHNIKOV: See the label?

VOLKOV: Of course, 'Genuine Kalashnikov vodka'. Do the Chinese copy this too?

KALASHNIKOV: Since I embraced the modern market system – at the insistence of my daughter – I've obtained a little revenue from products bearing my name. That's the best yet. The most useful, anyway.

VOLKOV: So, you don't benefit from arms sales, but you do benefit. As it were.

*Beat.*

KALASHNIKOV: A secret, comrade. Before long I'll be dead. What then? What will be left for Makka? A Hero's lot in the new Russia; a star on the chest and a black hole in the belly. Hup!

*KALASHNIKOV gestures for VOLKOV to toss it back. VOLKOV – being less confident – passes it over. KALASHNIKOV twists off the top and pours two shots.*

KALASHNIKOV: This provides some reward. No thanks to our friends, the English, who won't let it cross their borders: Unacceptable exploitation of weaponry. This from the invaders of Iraq. Your very good health, Volkov.

VOLKOV: And yours, General.

KALASHNIKOV: Misha.

*VOLKOV is incapable of calling him by his first name.*

VOLKOV: Dmitry.

KALASHNIKOV: If I remember, your father liked a drink.

VOLKOV: I thought you didn't remember.

KALASHNIKOV: A day in the woods. Names float back, faces. Technical solutions come together – crystallize in here. Often as not, with no conscious thought. That's how it's been today, for me and Nikolai Illyich Volkov.

VOLKOV: That's him. That's Papa.

KALASHNIKOV: Stoutish lad, dark features, quite tall.

VOLKOV: Yes!

KALASHNIKOV: Dim-looking. Comrades would pass Nikolai in the street, never a second glance.

VOLKOV: That's how he may have appeared.

KALASHNIKOV: Your Papa exaggerated our acquaintance. We passed the time of day, comrade to comrade, the odd drink.

Whatever happened to Nikolai, whatever you believe – I had no role in it. One day, the next, there, not there. Tunnel vision, back then, always. Even my own wife, my own children... Too busy putting a gun in Ivan's hands. I left the army, soon as I could, but with me it was always 'the project'. You do see that, Volkov?

VOLKOV: I know that, General.

KALASHNIKOV: Oh?

VOLKOV: My father's fall. That was his own doing. Papa was told a joke – this was 1948, or nine. How do we know Adam and Eve are good Party Members? One apple between two, barely a stitch for clothes, yet when arrested they still give their address as Paradise.

KALASHNIKOV: Ha! A good one!

VOLKOV: Papa thought so. He told the joke to the custodian of his building. She denounced him. It's probable that's who it was, he always thought so.

KALASHNIKOV: He found other work surely?

VOLKOV: Was given other work. Nikolai Ilyich was lucky. He survived.

KALASHNIKOV: Ah. Good. I remembered it right. Thank you, Dmitry Nikolaevitch.

*He embraces VOLKOV and kisses him. Then peals away.*

KALASHNIKOV: When I was a deputy I might have helped Nikolai, if he'd lived in our oblast, in Udmurtia, if I'd known he was suffering….

VOLKOV: General, are you alright..?

KALASHNIKOV: So – you are really here to interview Misha Kalashnikov.

VOLKOV: Yes, that's right.
Yes and no. I confess I have a special reason for seeking out the General. General.

*KALASHNIKOV smiles.*

KALASHNIKOV: I knew it. It's clear you're no journalist. Not the old school.

VOLKOV: Oh?

KALASHNIKOV: You haven't drained a glass since you got here. Is Dmitry Nikolaevich even a Russian, I wondered?

*He pours more – and downs it, feels it burning all the way down.*

VOLKOV: I'd like to show you some photographs. Still
   photographs, not film.

*Now KALASHNIKOV is hooked.*

KALASHNIKOV: Photographs? An invention, comrade? One
   of your own? I have to tell you Volkov, I don't have
   much influence with the patents office...

VOLKOV: These photographs were in my father's possession.
   He begged me to show them to you, one of the last
   things he said. By luck, this producer offered me
   expenses for an interview. You are six hundred miles
   from Moscow, and I am, well – divorce is not the
   earner you imagine.

KALASHNIKOV: Should have been a lawyer, mm? In
   America! Photographs. From the war years? From the
   Polygon?

VOLKOV: More recent. Not a place you've been to, I think.
   My father swore he would not have set foot there.
   Cursed me for doing so.

KALASHNIKOV: *(Now mystified.)* Photographs...?

VOLKOV: From a newspaper. My one big hit. Papa wangled
   the copies from the picture editor, an old friend, one of
   the few real friends my father had. It was he who got
   me the job, obviously. Trainee staff photographer.

*Beat. He produces an envelope, holding it as if it was Pandora's
box.*

*KALASHNIKOV is now wary.*

KALASHNIKOV: What happened to your hand, comrade?

VOLKOV: Nothing. Pest control.

*He passes the photos over.*

VOLKOV: One of my first assignments. The autonomous
   Russian Republic of Nagorno Karabakh, 1993. Winter

then. There's trouble in that hell-hole – where's Volkov?

*KALASHNIKOV begins to spread them on the table as best he can; automatically clicking into the task of organising them – sorting carnage from carnage.*

VOLKOV: There are two sets of pictures. The massacre of ethnic Azzeris by Armenians – the other set two months later, revenge attacks, Armenians slaughtered by Azzeris. 'An outbreak of extraordinary violence'. Pre-digital, we used film back then. I saw history repeat itself, right there in my sink.

KALASHNIKOV: We saw pictures like these on TV, Nonna and me. No Makka then – Elena wasn't even born. Unimaginable!

The beast of Nationalism unleashed – one tribe against the other. Gorbachev was too dim to see it coming. Before, we were united – all colours, all peoples, everyone – Slavs, Turkmen, Mongols, Tadjiks – all Soviets then, proud to be Soviets. Comrades, united, one flag, one society. Hopeless utopianism. Time to throw off the oppressive yoke of socialism. They were good days for me, Volkov, once Gorbachev got going. O yes, freedom? Free to travel. Little Misha, all over the world, mind expanding. Bulgaria first, then the rest. Here? At home? Disaster. Gorbachev, Yeltsin – idiots. Freedom to what? To regress, disintegrate, bestialize.

VOLKOV: Decapitate. That was the trend in Nagorno Karabakh – both sides – men, women, children – younger than Elena, younger than my girl now, full-clothed, perfect bodies all the way up to... *(The throat.)*... The rest dumped in the snow nearby. We called it a headshot.

KALASHNIKOV: Disintegration.

You must have had a strong stomach, Volkov, a steady hand, for this work.

*Beat.*

> So. This is what you wanted to show me? A Hero of
> Soviet Russia?

VOLKOV: The truth, emerging in my sink. Again and again.
Papa saw it straight away. Look – look closely General.
Look there.

KALASHNIKOV: War makes a beast of everyone.

VOLKOV: Weapons!! The assault weapon used by both sides.
AK-47s, sold on by Red Army conscripts.

KALASHNIKOV: Ah, you're right. Fancy. You can't blame
conscripts. Seventeen years old? Starving to death on
the front in some god-forsaken territory? Sell a gun for
a chicken when you're hungry, what lad wouldn't.

VOLKOV: 'These photos are all we have in common', he said.
Him at one end of the process, in the early days, me – I
fed off the results. I'd become a vulture. Vermin.

KALASHNIKOV: He was proud of you, I'm sure.
These are shocking pictures, Dmitry Nikolaevich. Very
sad.

*He passes them back to VOLKOV/walks away.*

VOLKOV: Papa made me swear I would pass on the message.
Tell Mikhail Timofeyevich, tell him I'm glad. Glad it
was the Kalashnikov, not my gun, that won the famous
competition. That it was Mikhail, and not Nikolai
who succeeded, who gave the world a weapon of such
pitiless, indiscriminate murder.

*Beat.*

KALASHNIKOV: He said what?

VOLKOV: 'Thank god it wasn't my rifle...'

KALASHNIKOV: Sorry comrade, that makes no sense.

VOLKOV: He meant, I believe… It's obvious…

KALASHNIKOV: Your father didn't have a rifle. He was on
    Simonov's team.
    Nikolai Volkov wasn't an inventor. Volkov! He was just
    a…just a…

VOLKOV: Just a man you wouldn't notice in the street.

KALASHNIKOV: An engineer. A comrade, for a while…

VOLKOV: Young socialist engineers, working together, just
    following orders.

*Beat.*

KALASHNIKOV: Now you listen to me Volkov. I designed a
    gun to fight the Nazis – to save Russia. It's not me puts
    them in the hands of ethnicidal maniacs. I don't run
    the shambles the army is today! Inventors design, that's
    all we do. Traders sell, politicians aim, people fire –
    soldiers *fire* guns, it's not me, it's not *soldiers*. Politicians
    deploy weapons, don't make that mistake.

VOLKOV: …and then there are the murderers, the gangsters.
    An international must-have for terrorists. Bin Laden
    himself never let himself be photographed without his
    AK. Do you know, Mikhail Timofeyevich, how many
    deaths are caused each year by what you worked, what
    you schemed to bring in to the world? An estimated
    three hundred and fifty thousand.

KALASHNIKOV: Estimated! Who estimates a thing like that?

VOLKOV: Nearly four hundred thousand – every twelve
    months.

KALASHNIKOV: My god, man…

VOLKOV: That's only… (an estimate).

KALASHNIKOV: …and how many are saved? Mm? Special
    services, domestic police forces. Plenty of them carry
    our weapons, did you think of that? We make work for

thousands of people. What about Libya? Gadaffi's still in power without my gun.

VOLKOV: Sixty years since the birth of the AK. How many lives did it save? In South Africa, to AK means to kill someone. Your name is a byword for death.

KALASHNIKOV: No no no no…

VOLKOV: That's why I had to seek you out.

KALASHNIKOV: That's not it…

VOLKOV: Why I came so far…(to find you).

KALASHNIKOV: Seek me out? Who said I was hiding? I retired, that's all I did, I live here by the lake…

VOLKOV: Find Kalashnikov. Warn him.

KALASHNIKOV: Warn him of what? I already know I'm dying!

VOLKOV: Your eternal soul, Mikhail Timofeyevich…I have to tell you, Your eternal soul is in peril.

KALASHNIKOV: Oh now you stop there. I let you into my house! Eat at my table… My daughter… Where is my daughter – *(Calling.)* Makka!!
I knew it! I'm not fearing you, 'Volkov', plenty of comrades have seen that face. I'm not so easy – now's my time is it?
Alright, Death. Or Death's agent, whoever you are, I'm ready. I warn you, I won't go easy. I can fight. I can defend myself.

VOLKOV: General, I would not have thought it of you.

KALASHNIKOV: No, so I imagine. Not many would.

VOLKOV: The arrogance!

KALASHNIKOV: Arrogance? You invaded my house, Volkov. You set the traps off. Volkov!! Wolf among chickens…?

VOLKOV: You think death comes to you…?

KALASHNIKOV: Comes to us all, I know that. I've nothing to be ashamed of. There's not many who can say that.

VOLKOV: Nothing to be…(ashamed of??!)

KALASHNIKOV: Saints and sinners? Not in my Russia. We make things, with our hands, things that work. We made a country out of nothing!
A patriot, that's what you found here, Death, nothing more. I've no secrets, nothing shameful…

VOLKOV: You don't see it! Death doesn't find you General. It goes out from you, it spreads across the world, floods of misery leak from you, like a…like a nightmare leaking…thing.

KALASHNIKOV: *(Enlightenment.)* Like a colandar…?

*Beat.*

KALASHNIKOV: *(Staying strong.)* No, no I was a soldier. Barely that – I left the army, got out, soon as I could. Tank sergeant? I'll be an inventor, help the world. It was Gorbachev made me a Captain. I was only made a General to make Yeltsin look like a president! I'm a civilian. A patriot, that's all you've got on me!

VOLKOV: Out, across the world. Wherever there's a conflict…

KALASHNIKOV: *(Failing.)*…like a colander under a tap.

VOLKOV: A dread, unstoppable thing. You're right, no journalist. Never a good one. *(He gestures to the photos.)* Flash in the pan. I should have had a t-shirt made: I got lucky in Nagorno Karabakh. A child's severed head, my lucky break. A mother's cry, noise in the head, forever.
I'm a messenger. That's all my work is, now. Deliver a simple message.

KALASHNIKOV: I worked to defeat fascism! Like building a Spitfire. Or an atom bomb!

VOLKOV: …and yet…

KALASHNIKOV: And yet nothing!

*Pause. VOLKOV is cowed, but not quite finished, his next line quiet.*

VOLKOV: There is…Jesus.

KALASHNIKOV: Like an atom bomb, like a Spitfire…

VOLKOV: Jesus forgives. That was Papa's message – the whole of the message. That's what he believed in the end – like so many in Russia now – what else is there? Like the Old Believers – something to cling to at the end of the world. Tell Kalashnikov – Jesus has the power to forgive. That's where his hope was – Papa's health broke long before yours, half your age. I'm glad he found something. I have nothing. Papa wanted his hero to know; You can be forgiven, absolved from your crimes, cleansed of your dreadful, dreadful mistakes.

KALASHNIKOV: Get out.

VOLKOV: My work is done. I can go.

*VOLKOV makes to leave, KALASHNIKOV is back at the photos.*

KALASHNIKOV: Wait. You answer a question from me, Death. You're the expert: how does a man take a woman's head off, a child's head? Eh, Death? How does he do it?

VOLKOV: I…I can't imagine…

KALASHNIKOV: A gun? – You weren't in the army, Dmitry Nikolaevich.

VOLKOV: Yes, yes…for a while.

*KALASHNIKOV goes to the shed, brings out a spade.*

KALASHNIKOV: Tools. The right tool for the job, every soldier knows that, an engineer, even a journalist knows that much. Here. See? A gun'll do it in the end, but why? Why use a rifle…? It's there, in your own pictures. A

spade, that's what you need. Blade above the neck –
both hands on the handle, straight down – chop. Seven
times, eight, even the kids, not like the movies, oh not
one clean swipe. No gun required; a heart of stone and
a good blade, that's all. Axe, chisel, spade. Chop. Chop.
Chop. Chop. Chop. Chop. Chop. Chop!

*He slings the spade aside.*

KALASHNIKOV: You should get back to Ngorno Kharabakh.
Better still, time travel. Find the first savage to smelt
iron. The first ape who bashed iron into a square and
nailed it to a staff. And you know what you should
do? Rip his heart out. Rip mine out too. My country
needed a gun, I made one. Do I tell Ivan who to fire at?
Do I tell these lunatics in Chechnya who to kill? Do I
wish I'd invented something else? Yes. A lawnmower.
Something for a farmer say, a chainsaw. Today in fact,
a helicopter. I could fly over this forest and find my
granddaughter, I am not able to do that!! Am I?! AM I,
Dmitry Nikolaevich?!! History gave me nothing!!

*Pause, as the penny drops in VOLKOV's mind, he glances toward the
wood, and tries vainly to frame the question. KALASHNIKOV – now
his secret is out – collapses onto a seat.*

*Enter MAKKA. She can't help but self-consciously tidy herself up a
bit, but in fact she is relaxed and bouyant.*

MAKKA: The wanderers returned did they?
Poor Papotchka, you'll be worn out. We were beginning
to give up hope.

*She kisses the top of his head.*

MAKKA: I'll sort some food out. If your boots are wet leave
them by the stove. Tell Elena to do the same. Dmitry'll
help me with the meal, won't you, Dima?
Dmitry will be staying Papa. If that's OK.

*Beat.*

MAKKA: What?

*Beat.*

VOLKOV: My work is done, I can go.

MAKKA: Have you two fallen out? Oh for goodness sake.
The only two men in miles and you're at each other's
throats. What is it, politics? If you're arguing about me,
I'll be very disappointed.
Where's Elena?
Papa?

*She stands in front of his face. She's still confident, relaxed, not
panicking.*

Papa – where did Elena go?
Papa? Look at me. IS YOUR BATTERY OUT, IS
THAT IT?
*(To no one in particular.)* Where is she?
*(To VOLKOV.)* Did you see her, Dima?
*(Calling.)* ELENA?
She hasn't gone off again?
Papa. PAPA!?
Papa, look at me. Papa?
Where's Elena? Where did she…

*Beat. Now the panic thuds in; she realises what the silence between
them means.*

She came back…?
Papa, she came back with you? PAPA! Papa you found
Elena.
PAPA TALK…(TO ME)

*KALASHNIKOV is on his feet.*

KALASHNIKOV: DON'T TREAT ME LIKE AN IDIOT!!
Elena's fine. She was on the ice, it's a game…

MAKKA: On the ice…?

KALASHNIKOV: I tracked her. By the time I got down
there she'd disappeared, she was gone, back into
the forest, bound to be... She's fine she's... She's got
the gun anyway...slipped back here...look, you see?
Classic manoeuvre. All the parts, taken... No one was
looking...no one noticed...

*It's true – the parts of the gun, so carefully laid out earlier, have
disappeared.*

MAKKA: Oh god.

Kalashnikov: She's armed, she'll be fine... She knows the
forest, like the back of her...

MAKKA: She's twelve years old!!

KALASHNIKOV: She's like a fairy, or a goblin, she's got no
enemies, a child like her...

MAKKA: She's got no...? Oh Christ! (The school).

*MAKKA's hand is over her mouth.*

KALASHNIKOV: Elena knows how to handle a rifle, I can tell
you that...

MAKKA: *(To VOLKOV.)* What are you doing? Why are you just
standing there? Go and find her!

VOLKOV: Right.

*VOLKOV glances towards the forest, but – ineffectual as ever – makes
no move.*

VOLKOV: Bears.
The General's right – she'll be fine.

*MAKKA walks very deliberately towards VOLKOV, and slaps his
face.*

VOLKOV: Makka, Makka Mikhailovna...

MAKKA: I'm going to phone – I'm going to find someone who
will help.

*Exit MAKKA. Pause.*

VOLKOV: You didn't find her. Since...

That's quite a time.

KALASHNIKOV: It's a game. If Elena isn't found believe me,
she doesn't want to be.

That's how children are, eh? They're born, they go
out, you've no control, you can't dictate. They change
– find new things, stupid things, silly, *opposite* things...
children, grandchildren...useless – wives? Like music
or the ballet – precious, not *useful*, not *practical*...

*He tears off his hearing aid.*

VOLKOV: Papa said the same. Useless.

KALASHNIKOV: *(Calling.)* YOU'RE WASTING YOUR
TIME MAKKA!

By the time anyone comes out here...

No one likes a joke more than Elena. Took your camera
too, d'you see?

VOLKOV: Oh god.

No no that's good. She...she's resourceful.

*He steps toward the forest again, but is too afraid to venture
further.*

KALASHNIKOV: She'll be back when it's over, when she's
done.

*KALASHNIKOV fumbles for the gear to make a cigarette.*

KALASHNIKOV: Makes me proud, knowing she's out there.
Facing down the enemy. Making the shadows shiver. A
proper Russian fairy.

*Snow begins to fall. The old man's hands are cold and clumsy.*

VOLKOV: Here, let me. LET ME.

KALASHNIKOV: I CAN MANAGE

VOLKOV: Please. PLEASE. I can do it. Let me. There, you
see.

*VOLKOV is now rolling the cigarette. He glances up at the drifting
flakes.*

VOLKOV: Almost Spring.

KALASHNIKOV: Snows in June, July. Freezes, thaws, freezes
thaws. The seasons toying with us, like the god no good
socialist believes in.

VOLKOV: Heavy, do you think?

KALASHNIKOV: Snow on snow, piling up. Never enough.

VOLKOV: Like that song you were singing. My mother sang
that song. Cover the tracks between my lover and
me…?

*They patch the song together between them, an attempt to keep
their spirits up, but it's pretty threadbare. VOLKOV has, meanwhile
perfected the roll-up – a more effective comfort.*

VOLKOV: Try that. Oh, here.

*He finds a lighter, but it won't spark. He throws it aside. Desolate, he
gently removes the cigarette from KALASHNIKOV's lips, straightens up.*

VOLKOV: It's going to be deep.

KALASHNIKOV: Never enough. Not now.

*VOLKOV glances round and picks up the spade. He runs his fingers
over the blade edge, and looks again towards the forest.*

VOLKOV: Little girl, in the snow.
I should go after her. Find her.

KALASHNIKOV: All the parts. Surrounded by space.
I was vrag naroda – enemy of the people.
The Motherland needed me.
What did I have to lose?

*Snow keeps falling. VOLKOV doesn't move. Lights fade, as screen lifes up.*

## 8

*Film: Side of the tool shed, screen. In the failing light of the woods, we see the camera is switched on. ELENA positions the camera, then shows us a number '8', drawn on her cardboard, and on the other side the legend, 'The Global Product'.*

*She tosses the cardboard aside, and drags the unzipped grip bag towards her.*

ELENA: This is it: the AK-47. It stands for Avtomat Kalashnikova 1947. They make thousands of these every week – millions in China, Pakistan, loads of places – but it still has just eight moving parts, like always. And it always always works.

*Inside the bag are the parts of the gun in a jumble. ELENA takes them out and assembles the gun, holding the parts to the camera.*

This is the main part, it's called the stock or receiver. Then you need the gas chamber…

This is the really clever part, the revolving breech block and carrier. A truly revolutionary innovation – twists the bullet just right. That goes next. Then the springy bit…

Where is it…there!

The return spring and rod: see? All joined together, so even an idiot can't lose it. But everything's on its own, separate, so nothing gets jammed. Smart.

Top cover…

Fore-rod, or cleaning rod…

And last you need the most important part – ammo. Yes!

*She attaches the magazine.*

To fire one shot, you push the catch here…and it's ready…

*She 'tracks' a 'target' with the gun, and pretends to fire off a single shot.*

Ker-blam!! Easy.

Or, you can shoot all the enemy at once. Want to punch the new girl now? I push the switch up, and… six hundred and fifty bullets a minute, rip through the flesh.

*She 'fires' again, mowing down the enemy.*

na-ha-ha-ha-ha!

*Beat. ELENA sniffs, and comes closer to the camera. She is now very calm and thoughtful.*

Or maybe I'll just kill a bear.

*She pushes the catch back to single shot.*

'Coming Bruno, ready or not'.

Granddad would like that, before he goes back to God.

*It's clear she knows KALASHNIKOV is dying.*

'Big people always underestimate little people'.

That's why the AK is so good – evens things up a bit. That's what all the little people should do. Swap a chicken for one of these...

*She primes the gun, and looks directly into the camera.*

…and the future is ours.

*The command 'Upload Now' flashes on the screen. ELENA reaches forward...*

*The screen snaps to another child, of a different race, also with an AK-47.*

*This is repeated, getting faster and faster and faster, mixing kids and adults… The noise gets louder and louder – achieving close-quarters volume, and is then cut dead.*

*Film: We are back in the forest, it is silent as the snow falls. We are watching ELENA as she steals through the trees, tracking her prey.*

*Fade to Blackout.*

*Music…*

*The End.*

# Appendix

*Under White Snow*

Do you remember,
Do you remember?
Two paths were joined, two lovers made their vow

Do you remember?
all the shooting stars
and our footprints lost beneath the fall of snow

Do you remember?
all those shooting stars
and our footprints lost beneath the fall of snow

Do you remember
Words that were spoken?
So hushed, the snowflakes swirling everywhere
Are they forgotten,
all your secret words
all the promises of love that touched my ear?
Are they forgotten,
all your secret words
all the promises of love that touched my ear?

Dear, I am waiting,
my heart is broken
I stand here so alone, and feel afraid

Calling and calling
O my love come quick
– but the tracks are gone, our love has lost its way
Calling, calling
O my love come quick
– but the tracks are gone, our love has lost its way

Do you remember,
love in December?
Two paths were joined, two lovers made their vow
Fast as a moonbeam
and the shooting stars
all our footprints lost beneath the fall of snow
Fast as a moonbeam
and the shooting stars
all our footprints lost beneath the fall of snow

# OTHER FRASER GRACE TITLES

### Frobisher's Gold
£8.99 / 9781840027099

### King David, Man of Blood
£8.99 / 9781849430333

### Breakfast with Mugabe
£8.99 / 9781840026306

### The Lifesavers
£8.99 / 9781840029178

### Perpetua
£7.99 / 9781840021226

# WWW.OBERONBOOKS.COM